REEL TO REAL

Reel to Real

Carroll Blair

Aveon Publishing Company

Copyright © 2012 by Carroll Blair

(First edition, Mellen Poetry Press)

All rights reserved. No part of this book may be reproduced, or transmitted in any form or by any means, electronic or mechanical, including photocopy, recording, or by any information storage and retrieval system without prior permission of the publisher.

ISBN: 978-1-936430-00-0

Library of Congress Control Number
2011961146

Aveon Publishing Co.
P.O. Box 380739
Cambridge, MA 02238-0739 USA

Also by Carroll Blair

Grains of Thought
Facing the Circle
Shifting Tides
Reaches
Out of Silence
Quarter Notes
By Rays of Light
Into the Inner Life
Gnosis of the Heart
Soul Reflections
Beneath and Beyond the Surface
Of Courage and Commitment
For Today and Tomorrow
In Meditation
Sightings Along the Journey
Through Desert's Fire
Offerings to Pilgrims
Human Natures
(Of Animal and Spiritual)
Atoms from the Suns of Solitude
Colors of Devotion
Voicings

Contents

Part I

Peaceably Ending 3
Pictures from a Dream 4
Entropic Sensories 5
Flashes of Miracles 6
Love's Survival 7
But If All Came to Pass 8
In the Hour Uncertain 9
What Do They See 10
An International Affair 11
Stone Man 12
Miss H 13
Toward the Darkness 14
A World Unfolding 15
A Punishing of Self-Standing 16
Will You One Day Count for Something 17
Cosmic Fare 18
For Anything For 19
A Sad Thing I Saw Today 20
Moment of Joy 21
Spirit Awakening 22
Lone Deliverance 23
Lifetime 24
What Will It Be 25
Changes 26
On This Last Day of Summer 27

The Bird and the Bees	28
A Fugitive's Heart	29
Melody	30
Everything Has Eyes (or so it seems)	31
Fate and Destiny	32
Wind Is All You Shall Receive	33
A Hard Thing to Learn	34
Little Girl Across the Street	35
To Feel the Light	36
Invitation	37
I Would Believe	38
Sing to Me Not	39
Motion of Truth	40
Show of Heart	41
Master of Servility	42
Earth Town Retreat	43
Yes & No	44
Blushing Pains	45
Meditation	46
The Greatest Lover of Life	47
Tragic Sense	48
Poem to Poem	49
The Damned	50
Response to the Holy	51
Never to Cease	52
Insulting the Day	53
Question to a Philosopher	54

Part II

Surprise 57
M & M 58
It's the Look That Counts 59
From the Personals 60
Nursing a Cold to Its Demise 61
Physician X 62
Nothing to Nowhere 63
The New Age 64
A Child of God 65
Face to Faith 66
Something Anyway 67
What Good the Love 68
Mistaken Identity 69
Imagine 70
Arrival 71
No Questions Please 72
Contemporary Lawsuit 73
Song in the Rain 74
She Has It 75
What Next 76
Understanding 77
Hello – Reality – Goodbye 78
Lost Emotion 79
Honey of the Muses 80
Journey of Progress 81
List of Things to Do When You're Bored 82
Search of a Clever-Crazy 83
Painted Ivories 84

Opinion	85
Foreign Steps	86
The Longest Marriage	87
Excerpts from a Sage's Diary	88
Parting Question	89
Before You Were Before	90
A Father's Hope	91
In Shadow	92
No Not Want to Know	93
The Man Who Couldn't Wait	94
Killing Spree	95
Absent Authority	96
In Mo(u)rning	97
Empty Eyes	98
World Song	99
Truce	100
Where Lightning Strikes	101
Waiting for the Lightning	102

I

Peaceably Ending

Half past the midnight
of Turbulence-d Blessed
I watch with aching eyes
to see what might have missed
the porch light
brightening to the flutter
of a moth on its way
to its death
stopping briefly, beautifully
to dance a cool hymn
in mid-air for a kiss
of the porch light
now fading to the sigh
of a moth peaceably
                    ending

Pictures from a Dream

A proud consistency pursuing a coda
not yet ready to place its stamp on
the roundabout finale of a dream —

An orchestra drunk with boredom —
Taps filling the hall —
A child playing in the balcony —

A mouse in tuxedo pulls the curtain
missing the conductor by a tick of the clock —

The audience refusing to leave

Entropic Sensories

Groomed rituals sewn in gullible fashion

Shoes tidy, no bear to fit
its paw

A kangaroo lash in the soup

Three sins for the broth up
to a jaded cross
finely timed for a savior's call —

Blue spasms choked by the hour
skins crawl
not worried at all
The lion's sure to show —

Packed pictures primed for a Slit-V
The day bruised by yellow leaves
strict in entropic sensories

    for

        the

Extraordinarily ordinary men flying
in barrels
(A cape for a friend?)

No prize for the Zero painting tattoos
on the wind.

Flashes of Miracles

I have seen
 in flashes
  of miracles
too shy
 to express
  themselves,
curses
 more
  beautiful
   than
the
 thought of
  the sun
   falling
    clean

Love's Survival

In the crosswinds of desert silence
green feet step to the dance
without warning escaping
a deep suffering bound to
an enterprise sealed in secrecy.

An end has not been created
for the story that weeps
without end—that bleeds
forcefully beneath wounds
that will not heal for the
sake of Love's survival

But If All Came to Pass

But if all came to pass in
the still dawn unending
in its longing for angelites
weak in synchronized faith
abashed by the jaws of life's
brute force in changings
calcified for a parched-blue
rain spoiled by the sneeze
of a butcher's flu in
tripled tragedy counting its
victims by the laughter of
Promise glued to a destiny
unfit for all who reign
by a thread crossed by
Time's velvet deceits cloaked
in serial dread could you
still feel the absurdity of
tem-p-o-r-al be-i-ng

In the Hour Uncertain

Where the streets merge like rivers
on their way to eternity, and
owls scare the tigers dressed in
crayon suits, and faces never
changing in a sea of scattered
emotion drool at the feet of
loved ones, and churches without
gods sing to the heavens fixing
themselves to a prayer that
yearns without pause . . .
Here, in the hour uncertain
crushed like lamps invisible
a choice leaps in immaculate
force guiding destinies to their
ports watched by seals mourning
sworn to the mystery of life-
begets-life blessing candles in the
distance with the flaps of their
flippers, asking their guests to
turn off the TV.

What Do They See

What do the creatures who dwell at the
very bottom of the seas see in a
darkness darker than the darkest
space of the heavens

(Perhaps more than any man
has ever seen —)

An International Affair

The guests sang attentions in closing
a cappella furthering rumors slated for
the cereal box in yesterday's print —
Assailants kidnapped the rabbit of
a prince leaving its cage spinning
in the lobby its capped teeth stuck
to the nylons of a maid in cap and
gown — a flash seen round the world
the hotel was up in arms, cameras blinding
reporters rushing to the story gorging on
redbones fleeced from the Eiffel Tower —
It was an international affair

Stone Man

Crouched in a corner of the world
a stone man sleeps dreaming of
bold infinities colliding in dancing
shapes and colors fighting to be
free of each other, to be free of
themselves longing to die in a
peace that only stone men can
dream of.

Miss H

You bore articles from your breasts
like foaming children needless
in a cream-colored dream
not reducible to a stream
of mistrustful tears.
Shunned early of aspirations peeling
from the tact of a hound you wound
yourself in naked testaments to
the point of poignant delays
boarding liners in the desert set
for a pursuit of ancient diseases,
pedant rituals dividing your course
in three semesters memorized
by the about-face of a smile
stuck frozen in proud simplicities
sorting principles with letters to
the Sphinx between their teeth.

The hour was ripe for a carpet
madam waxed lightly at the knees
to burn the ashes of fine tales
before a jar of vinegar (the gods
love pretty knees) activating
full charge the silent symphony
moaning between her legs —

firelust beneath the snow

Toward the Darkness

Running toward the darkness
forgetting everything to learn
the All of Nothing I cross the
River of Lethe without stopping
to drink of its waters. It is
disappointed, but waits for
my return . . .
(It knows I *must* return.)

A World Unfolding

A tossed horizon groping for the
sun lost in a game of hide and
seek and hide with the moon
two stories from a myth shaved
to its naked bones.

Silence caked with gunpowder shot
deep from a cannon without eyes,
its black iron sneezing in the rain
blowing Hope into fragments up and
away into the heart of a tangerine
sky where beauties laugh in a
joy-dance of despise, despising a
warrior's sentiments closing in on
a seasoned tide promised to a
world unfolding.

A Punishing of Self-Standing

A punishing of self-standing standing
in the murky depths of mysterious
occasion proceeding unseen
to unknowables thirsting to
a climb of attending resolution.

Postures erupt in address to
plural gravities consumed by
linear dread —

A recognition of esteem extending its
story ashen to fouled exigencies . . .
a shredding of funeral arrangement.

Will You One Day Count for Something

Will you one day count
for something in this
closet of troops bashing
termites with bored mallets
hurrying the next meeting
of seconds not disturbing
the shades wrapped in
a corner of dust playing
dare-games with loose
matches striking a pose
for the favor of comfortable
clothing scaring moths into
the pockets of mad troops
circling the darkness
waiting for a broom
to fall

Cosmic Fare

It is there, all there for the
taking . . . The glass slippers
you promised to the moon
dancing to curiosities on
strings of fire; the elephant
flying in its sleep lying
in the street with pink stories
tied to its ears slapping the tar
with its trunk; the cases of love
brought in by trucks from a
distant star breathing heavily
from the heat of its light;
the wolf songs, the fables,
and all singular details
forcing the throat of Reality
to sing its calloused hymns
on the laps of children who
hold Fate in the palms of
their hands chanting to the crawl
of a spider on its way to cities
dying in a mass of diseased
perception, carrying green bibles
to the corners of their grave.

For Anything For

Anything for a laugh, a cry,
a wonder-why;

the shattering of illusion

a flag flying in the wind

A Sad Thing I Saw Today

... a man who couldn't write his name.

Moment of Joy

An old man sits in the shade
beneath a tree in his years
seated in a white folding chair;
he is eating grapes, their purple
sweetness staining his aged hands —
he smiles, not every tooth of
his youth present to join in his
joy. He looks up at the sun
that cannot find him; then,
observing a cloud drifting away,
he hears his son call to him:
"Father, it is time to come in."

He stays in his chair for another
moment, eating his grapes, for
another moment, where (for a
moment) both sun and son
will not find him.

Spirit Awakening

By the light of two prison-ed
wings a truth stands guard as
a faithful servant guarding the
sickbed of his master.

Stroked in armored sensory
aligned to a bilious claim
a deviled heart bids for the pain
that shivers the soul without
care or warning; that greets the
shadowed wall of Awakening with
the sting of a serpent's kiss.
No rejection may be accepted at
the time of its call—at the
sacred hour of Stand or Fall

Lone Deliverance

An isolation caught in the throat
thrashed violently at words yearning
to break through to a thousand
targets begging for an assault —
Goose bumps told the story of
grenades faltering in their game,
of ruined autopsies, of corroded
madnesses sealing to a fate
unresolved in raging hands; of
sodium troops screaming for the
raid they were denied forced to
retreat to blind spaces torturing
in their silence —

The always more than prayer for
a creed of sorcery seeking powers
primed to a fever's pitch, panting
in scores of fury bound to a bliss
true to its cause of breaking
through to the mission of lone
deliverance, seizing sole dissonance
divine

Lifetime

It takes a lifetime to say
when one has nothing to say,
and still all cannot be said

What Will It Be

The world
perpetually spinning on the tip
of God's finger . . .
Will first His finger tire,
or will boredom
overtake Him
before
He flicks the world
into the
abyss
and start anew

Changes

Changes made — man-made — for
this, for that, for everything
under the sun —
The sun burning with indifference

On This Last Day of Summer

Into the street a ball bounces
escaping from the joy of a child —
a car brakes to a halt though not
in time, killing the ball in its
track — The ball, dead, murdered
in the street, so still and lifeless in
the street. A second car restores its
life with a clumsy sorry-I-didn't-
mean-it thud —
The ball bouncing back to the child

The Bird and the Bees

I tell you I saw it . . .
a bird speaking to a colony
of bees in chirping dialect
scolding in a manner any
preacher would be proud of:
"What do you think you're doing?
Stop that buzzing around my
space that extends for a mile
in all directions — make your
honey elsewhere, and don't expect
flowers on the queen's birthday.
Now shoo, all of you, and the
soldiers of your colony know
what they can do with their stingers."

Now I'm as sure of this as I am
sure of anything. Though I must
confess that I am sure of nothing;
but the bees never did return, and
the bird chirps each morning perched
on a branch all his own in the
apparent joy of his solitude.

A Fugitive's Heart

In company not suited to a
fugitive's heart, pain licks the
atmosphere with omnivorous lust

The cold silence testifying
in the air

Melody

It doesn't take much for a melody
to turn into a song; but for it
to *sing* . . . in music, words, or
just plain living —
That is another matter, another
story, another . . . melody

Everything Has Eyes (or so it seems)

Everything has eyes, or so it seems . . .
The rock inviting the wave to splash
upon it, the wave never missing its
mark; the tree swaying in seduction
drawing the swallow to nest upon
its branches; sky, wind, cloud,
moving to the rhythms of a cosmic
design they seem to know something
about (or at least more than any man);
plants turning toward the sun; bats
as blind as the wisdom of the fox;
Will, pulsing invisible through every
atom invisible, moving the whole
body of Existence onward from one
moment to the next with a grace of
command no blindness could ever achieve —

Everything has eyes, or so it seems . . .
(at least to those who have eyes)

Fate and Destiny

If you did absolutely nothing,
Fate would still come to claim
you, but Destiny would be waiting
in the distance like an impatient
master with arms folded tapping
his foot, staring without a blink

Wind Is All You Shall Receive

You who stand beneath the
falling rains of Pity waiting
still to receive the praises
of hearting angels . . .
The gods will not send them —

wind is all you shall receive

A Hard Thing to Learn

To

    leave

        that

            which

                lies

   dying

       in our

            lives

   to

      die

         in

           peace

Little Girl Across the Street

There's a little girl outside my window;
she's standing across the street. A beautiful
child, about six years old. She is waiting
for the school bus, dressed in a white
sweater, a pink dress, white shoes and pink
socks with a book bag strapped to her back
and a lunch box in her right hand.
It's a beautiful fall morning (September)
and she looks more than beautiful just
standing there waiting for her bus.

With her free hand she brushes away
the long yellow hair that the wind has
gently placed upon her face.

A cat approaches her.
She bends down to pat it.
The cat runs away . . .

There's a little girl outside my window,
a beautiful child

. . . .   I wish her a happy life

To Feel the Light

To feel the light reflecting in
the room with one's mind; its
warm simplicity tickling senses
not identified setting thoughts in
motion to broad invisibles . . .
A sharpening of awareness does not
reveal itself, but a feeling insists
it is there probing the nature
of dimensions inexplicable, so
subtle in the taunt of their mystery

Invitation

Three phrases stalk the corridors
of my heart listening with cool
hesitance to an invitation whispering
from the corners of the world
(what world — my world).

Centered in calibrations dark and
finely tuned to the forces that pull
me here and there and there
they are ready to do the necessary
of spilling their message before
judge and jury knowing two
will be sentenced to death,
one granted the life of a
butterfly crowned king for a
day over the dominion of the world
(what world   my world).

I Would Believe

And yes, if you would understand
as much; and yes, if you would
go to the dream of bold definition
with dark appearance moving clean
with leopards on your back, and
circle the moon with your thoughts
while tasting a rainbow with your
tongue, and stick branches between
your words and carry them to the
edge of the earth setting candles
along the way forgiving everyone
for their crimes against you except
those who have loved you

I would believe what you say you believe

Sing to Me Not

Do not sing to me your frivolous
songs of joy rehearsed from the
cellars of faint hearts —
You are all too young or too old
in experience to touch the melody
of *real* joy; out of reach to all but
a few who have suffered at degrees
of intensity far beyond the capacity
of your imaginations to fathom —
No, do not sing to me nor speak to me
of your joy too weak to speak for itself —

Motion of Truth

Truth moves in features unrecognized
from the angle of swollen comfort,
or is it false address? Revealing a shade
of itself only to one who is willing to pay
dearly for it — For it, for it will, for it
will not, will surely NOT be swayed
in its manner of pleasured crucifixions
dazzling the eyes of spectators (stupid
spectators) drooling with fevered lust
for a soon-to-bleed victim

Show of Heart

Once there was a band of grateful travellers stretching their thanks to the heavens, filled with rejoice for having missed a catastrophe they just barely escaped. But their rejoicing was premature, for suddenly a tremor shook the ground startling them, causing an exodus toward a mountain that fumed No Trespassing! Frightened and confused about what was happening and the uncertainty of where they were going, they stopped moving a short distance beyond the point of their departure and joined in a circle to hold hands and pray to a god — any god that might hear them and make their believed fortune more than just a dream, but their prayers went unanswered. One of them stepped out of the circle saying "Follow me, and I will free you from your fear," but no one dared to follow. He then went on his own; those who stayed behind perished in their place, as did the one who went on alone — but he perished on top of the mountain that fumed No Trespassing!

Master of Servility

He knows his way out, the drunken
servant too frightened to sober up
and march his masters out of his
life and rule over his own destiny
and destroy categories strapped to
his mind by murderers of his youth
and fight to the death if need be with
any fool who ever again comes along
and tries to tell him what to do, and
stand boldly before the sun shaking
his fist with pride and curse the
shaming sin of cowardice long controlling the reins of his being what being
lost being (found being) and grab his
demons by the throat and bid them
to dance Command them, to *dance* . . .

Earth Town Retreat

Meek figures dining in compartments
reserved for a king — king to a city
torn by centuries of everything
going to hell.

Striking devils sweep garbage at
one's feet complaining never about
the filth they encounter daily to
their loved ones, responding to laws
suitable for a terminal subway
loyal to its shrine of Modernity.

Yes & No

These are the words that
disturb the peace
of IS —
That shadow the gray light
of Reality
cold without repentance.

Blushing Pains

Blushing pains beginning the
crawl of mightly journeys
tortured in bliss
forever sworn to the
grail unidentified
seeing nothing of all
that is not to be
for everything the day
to grant its light to
blushing pains unending

Meditation

In and out of a labyrinth
fleeting without a surface
without a center rising
in hidden clarities unseen
never found never grasped
a roving eye determined in
its task to find to find a scrap
of something certain solid definitive
matchless in its surety if not its purity
snatched from the depths of a universe
unsavory in its manner of being.

The Greatest Lover of Life

"The hell with it all," he said; —
"Let the stupidities of the world
tear all reason to shreds and its evils
spew their poisons so thoroughly that
not one particle escapes their venom.
I'm done playing the fool trying to do
something about it. You conquer one
stupidity and two new ones appear
ready to taunt and torment and do
their mayhem, or pin one evil to the mat
and ten more come rushing to its aid.
No — no — Enough!" he said . . .
"Let the stupidities of the world
rip all sanity to pieces and its evils
wrap around the heart of goodness
like crushing serpents squeezing its
life into oblivion and end this sorry mess."
Turning away from his thoughts
he faced the sunset and began to weep.

Tragic Sense

I understand now your tragic sense
in the highest sense of its lowliness
of its loneliness curled up in a ball
inviting the world to play with it —
four stories old it sings with bitters
in its throat the most beautiful song
I've ever heard.

Poem to Poem

There is a shortage of wet
feet; the ducks are afraid
to go into the water —
the weeds, cutting like glass
through flesh, like pain through the heart
growing in calm and insight — the eyes
of the cleverest duck fast to the one
in the bush who wants to kill him

The Damned

I have seen the damned,
they will not grow;
beetles crawl on their hands
for attention, they can give
them nothing but love

Evil knows their weaknesses,
it will not attack;
it hates them too much for that

Response to the Holy

A response to the Holy
brief in its moment of communion
speaking worlds
by the prism of its light
pointing the way
to the Temple of Lost Truths —

A staff of gold rising from the mud

an infant sleeping by the door

the sun missing a pair of bloody shoes

Never to Cease

Fools wailing from the basement
of man's soul nickeling and dimeing
their way to the entrance of Escape
promising to take them as far as
their wits will carry them.

They shall never leave, and the
wailing shall never cease.

Insulting the Day

Calling the day over before it is over,
insulting its last hours with fatigue
that hasn't been earned —
not a deed or even a moment
notable nor memorable as payment
for its blessings; only a rude gratitude
from the bleachers of contempt.

Question to a Philosopher

Who do you think you are, sitting there
in the shade reflecting on the makeup of our
lives and its matter-of-fact spurious state
stealing our secrets with your eyes
cold like the skin of a snake god

II

Surprise

Caught by Surprise *again*, that cunning devil
master of the tease showing up at the most
unexpected times in the most unexpected places
with the manners of a prince who hasn't been trained,
but intelligent, so intelligent like the inventors of
chess and canned tuna playing games with the witted
and witless defeating all, never a loss to show for its
something more and less than trouble seated at the
back of its schemes planning Wonder and Mayhem
for its victims working nonstop round the clock
like old St. Nick on Christmas Eve

M & M

The mistake of many marriages exhibited so well
illuminated by many of their offspring—mistakes
manifested as the result of a mistake mistaken in
the identity of the true measure of the mistake
overlooked by other mistakes caught in the thick of
their own creation of additional mistakes—That is,
if there is really free will behind all that we do and
there is no rhyme or reason or nonsense or stupidities
(or mistakes) until we commit ourselves to action
setting ourselves in motion, doing what we want to
what we choose to, creating our own destinies and
shaping our own lives as we go along — If not,
and all is predetermined, as good as written in stone
since the Big Bang, then all is meant to be, and this
poem is a mistake.
(But if all is meant to be how can this poem be a
mistake? Unless the Big Bang was a mistake —
Then everything is a mistake the errors manifest
of one huge mistake.)

Am I mistaken?

It's the Look That Counts

And now, finally for the first time
in your life Sensation has met its
deadline gluing emotions together from
fragments of maturities and immaturities
like the model airplane you built for the
class project (needed by Friday must be in
by Friday) looking good but unable to fly.
"That's OK, it's alright, you see it's the
look that counts" whispered everywhere
(*everywhere*) . . . but only in silence

From the Personals

Oh just when you thought you were coming
into my life ready to set up house and put in
a garden and change the wallpaper, the rugs,
the phone number, the clocks, add a dog and
a couple of cats, paint the mailbox and throw
out the pictures with the trash I stopped you
in your tracks and sent you packing.

My heart decided to go with you.

Now I don't know where to find you
to retrieve my heart.

Nursing a Cold to Its Demise

Hot
soups
plenty of
rest
no sex
no
cartoons
no
thoughts
that
spit
at
the moon

Physician X

With stony eyes he scans the files of his patients,
profit traced upon his brow flipping pages from
a patient's file looking to see what coverage
there might be, his waiting room near full,
his heart near empty, his mind somewhere in
between wondering what fee he may charge
for his less-than-excellent services
delivered with ego unceasing.

Nothing to Nowhere

A loathing cruising the assembly line denting six cans
a signature of contempt—foremen spitting coffee in
each other's faces slowly getting around to plans of
speeding up production the god of the century
workers working to work to work to work their souls
to the bone so their bodies won't go hungry and their
minds won't go brilliant their TVs and video games
will see to it, compliments of their paychecks made
possible by their timecards checked three times by
their boss, sometimes by the boss of their boss their
anxiety about job security increasingly insecure also
making a generous contribution to their waning
quality of being, not noticeable to the point of
broadcast-appearance to the pronouncement of lost
identity fatigue veiling the curse of their plight
ennui pulling the crime over their hearts
the nothing-to-nowhere
over their eyes

The New Age

Born
this morning
bristling
with
promise
(so much
promise)
crushed
by a
prophet
in
Nike shoes

A Child of God

He left a raven at the altar with
the Holy Ghost to feed on circles
of yeast half in the mold —
A disturbance came from the balcony;
no choir rehearsal that day . . . just the saints
washing the floors with their tears

Face to Faith

What else could it do, the fine misfortune stealing an airplane to crash into a cloud (not just any cloud one with faces on it) swirling to a dive impressive to delirious spectators expecting nothing, less than nothing really from anything their eyes happened to set upon, the airplane smashing through the cloud wiping the faces off its smile on its way to crashing into onlookers' dreams heads up, now down tucked between their shins preachers darting out of the way for Lucy dear Lucy, so pleased to let the games begin.

Something Anyway

"It's something anyway"; something, they said
for the trouble of life . . . a tip for the gravedigger
paid in advance — the washbowl's free of blood
today, the sparrows went unfed, and all that was
heard from the Greeding Gallery was a chorus of
knocking knees waiting for a peace to take them away

What Good the Love

What good is the love incapable of reaching
into the depths of another's soul; scratching at
the surface of a life with a strength no greater
than a kitten's paw; a courage no grander than
the follow-the-crowd-like-everyone-else character
impressed with the surface of things, the appearance
of things, unable to get behind them, beneath them,
beyond them; insulting Love's integrity by speaking
its name in a manner of loose change . . .

What good the love such love, if it indeed be love —
(The 'love' that all but few harbor within)

Mistaken Identity

A. "Are you not a little ashamed that you exist?"

B. "No."

A. "Embarrassed?"

B. "No! Why do you ask?"

A. "I thought you were a spirit of high order; one of true substance and worth. All such spirits are somewhat ashamed of their existence. Please forgive my erroneous assumption."

B. "Wait! Wait! I am ashamed. I am!"

A. "But now you are ashamed because you've never been ashamed, and I am ashamed for provoking your shame, and we stand in embarrassment before each other for the same reason: the mistaken opinion that we both had pertaining to your worth."

Imagine

(Imagine) all those nasty things being said
about us sticking stubborn to the roof of Truth
like that—stubborn like molasses on a winter's
morn what is there to say? But wouldn't a calendar
pinup look fine (just fine) there hanging from
the light of her photograph

Arrival

A man sixty-five years, four months,
nine days, thirteen hours, twenty-five
minutes and thirty-seven seconds old
walks into a corner store —

It took him sixty-five years, four months,
nine days, thirteen hours, twenty-five
minutes and thirty-seven seconds to
get there (and Existence more than
thirteen billion years to prepare the event).

No Questions Please

"I welcome you home from your life.
We will need you to fill out a questionnaire
telling us what you've been doing there,
in your life . . . your comings and goings;
your activities, your associations, the places
you've been, the things you've done; what
you have seen, touched, tasted, smelled, heard
about, talked about; the things you loved, despised,
considered and denied; what you feared for and
cared for; who you were kind to, cruel to, fair
and unjust to; your hopes, your dreams, your
triumphs and your defeats; what you believed in,
who you confided in; the things you created and
destroyed; the known results of your good and
your evil; the forces that shaped you, encouraged
you, drove you to si.."

    "Where am I? What is this place?
    Are you an angel or a devil?"

    "No questions please."

Contemporary Lawsuit

It was like this, see; he was looking for
a punch in the nose, so I hit him — I
missed his nose and hit his head. His head
didn't break, but my hand did. I am now
suing him for damages resulting from the
provocation that compelled me to hit him,
an act which caused the fracture of my
hand—the blame of course resting entirely
on the one who provoked the incident.
Do you see the logic in this?

No matter —
      See you in court

Song in the Rain

Who are these people singing in the rain
so proudly singing and dancing, now laughing
snatching lines from a movie screen
frozen on a ceased-to-be Hollywood lot
the streetlights complementing the show of
kings who were toads just moments ago

She Has It

Yes, the glass look of beauty
too fragile to touch.

Flowers in a vase sigh on
her table as she longs for
the one who will take her
and feed her to the wolves

What Next

Auras, jellyfish, truths with no skeletons

a dandelion growing on the backstairs

rats finding love in the cellar

(what will the gods think of next?)

Understanding

It's understood now the knotting gaze you gave
the first time you left in your mannequin suit not
to return until noon the next day the next to the last
day of that savior's death scolding the neighborhood
with his departure leaving traces of our sins in the
snow melting slowly, deliberately by the worthy
and not so worthy sorting fragments of rhyme
clawing at the threads of worn meanings too late
to save the promise that came of its own accord

Hello – Reality – Goodbye

Go now . . . move your life into a world
waiting to receive you, but doesn't need you.
Make your presence *felt*, at least to yourself.
A great deal of unintentional planning
has brought you here—but remember,
the world doesn't need you.
(It's important that you remember this)

Lost Emotion

A lost emotion coming back to haunt
coming back to taunt in several phases
staking its claim on the heart of its victim
ill with the curse-gift-curse of seeing all —
A veil to trick the approaching pain —
another truth is coming to torture . . .
welcome, child, to the s-p-i-r-i-t-o-l game

Honey of the Muses

Drip

        Drip

                Drip
falls the honey

    of the Muses

        blessing their subjects

with sweet kisses

                of Immortality —

But the price . . . oh the price . . .

Journey of Progress

America's journey of progress travelled on the road
of the never-ending bill, of the all dollar mighty
stepping on the face of old George W.
along the way *all* the way

(It's not what he had in mind)

List of Things to Do When You're Bored

Throw scrambled eggs at the refrigerator —
Kiss the mailman —
Take ballet lessons in the Bronx —
Snarl at the next news anchor that invades your living room then pour corn oil on the TV —
Go shopping with a state trooper —
Sing a beautiful song in the ugliest place you can find —
Paint an ugly picture in the most beautiful place you can find —
Ride a donkey into the desert and eat a scorpion —

Search of a Clever - Crazy

A clever-crazy stuck his eye in the belly of
a bluefish searching for lost hooks believing
the hook lost superior to the hook new—almost
divine like a sacred relic frozen in the image of
Truth times two this belief stamped on all quarters
of his mind as he stared deeply into the belly of
a bluefish searching for lost hooks.
He found nothing but blood and guts —

In the shape of a hook

Painted Ivories

How pure the painted ivories
carry in semblance a souled
benevolence dispersed in shading
light left to answer
unanswerables to all voices
calling at the Hour of Summary

Opinion

OPINION — as hard as rock —
as contrived as salt —
a fusion of conceptions
conceptualized in a stream of
biased sensories giving slight attention
not sensitive less wise to the opulent
shades of opposings cutting their path
to the quiet flame of IS
nibbling the ear of Influence with
black teeth prepared to draw blood
if necessary at any moment   necessary

Foreign Steps

He speaks in foreign languages,
she dances in foreign steps,
stepping on the words she doesn't
understand and more than understands,
so subtle in her grace to the words
she mocks in time, and the he she
does not rhyme.

The Longest Marriage

The marriage of Knave and Fool —
the longest marriage in history . . .

ten thousand years and no divorce pending

Excerpts from a Sage's Diary

Running back and forth between the
mundane and profound, need and want
torching my back burning my eyes
never a moment's peace, wouldn't mind
stopping dead in the middle smack dead
in the center of Life's center and welcome
the angel of death to come . . .
Angel, are you listening?

*   *   *   *

I have my dreams, and my gratitude,
and my senses dedicated to my torments
sold to worlds uncompromised, and the promise
of strife waiting at the end of the rainbow
with scarred feet and hands —

a face that can't be seen

*   *   *   *

Transient beauties making their way to
my soul; I will not allow it —
Away from the path that has prepared
for the Eternal. Mock as you retreat
if you please, if you will, but away from
the path that has prepared for the Eternal —

*   *   *   *

Only the blind run toward the light
with eyes wide open and head upright.

*   *   *   *

Parting Question

A. "Is this all there is to life?"

B. "Yes. For you, this is all there is to life."

A. "And not for you?"

B. "No."

A. "Why is this all there is for me but not for you?"

B. "Because I haven't asked the question."

Before You Were Before

Before you were a man you were a boy
you were an infant you were an embryo
you were an egg you were sperm you were
animal you were plant you were mineral
you were water you were gas you were
atom you were molecule you were nothing
you were . . . The Beginning

A Father's Hope

Leaning over the crib of his newborn son
looking at him without really seeing him,
too busy in his mind hoping the world
will be kinder to his child than it has been
to him, and wondering what he is dreaming
now at this moment . . .
    (the dreams, he hopes, of a king)

In Shadow

Eyes swollen with love too bruised to cry
peeking in shadows for the source of your
many tortures —
A phantom whispers the meaning of your name;
you smile and promise not to shame him

No Not Want to Know

They don't really want to know; no, not really what is troubling you and how your wings were clipped leaving you maimed in the dirt banished by unknowables left to scrape the scraps from the floor of Life's blessings — No, they are only too glad so glad that there is one less competitor in the race for glory, their ears too clogged with fractured applause to hear you calling from your quarters:

"That's not what I was after . . . That's not what I was after!"

The Man Who Couldn't Wait

Jumped headlong into the thick of it
traffic stopped cold, would've loved to
run him down if only they'd thought of it —
A cup for the blind strapped to his belt
(no time for hitting up tourists and sailors)
Gotta go gotta run to the uptown feel-around
bazaar for the bizarre ten stories above the
headline news — a frolicky start for the genius-fool
on his way to something new (no, not new just
something to do) the story of pin-to-the-ass-
moving-one-off-his-butt running from here
to there to who knows where for a ringside seat
to a sideshow this time at the uptown feel-around
bazaar for the bizarre ten stories above the headline
news —
(Make that twelve stories.)

Killing Spree

A killing spree bought and paid for by those less
likely to kill but enjoy the thrill of pain being
displayed at a distance, they safe and tucked away
somewhere far away from the sport of mayhem —
Spectators to the last cell of their bones their
pleasure pitched to the joy of abandoned bliss
their hearts ablaze with an excitement only the most
powerful sex could equal in fervor as they sit rapt
like emperors watching the last Christian being
mauled by lions red grapes held lightly in their hands
death moans sighing in the throat
Evil laughing in the wind

Absent Authority

With chalk in hand he scrawls on the blackboard
scrawling without authority his chalked-white fingers
scribbling without conviction nothing strong enough
in his words (now the blackboard's words) to keep
the class interested in the history of the free world
on this first day of school imprisoned in their seats
the playthings of bureaucrats and mediocrities
for the next three seasons.

In Mo(u)rning

The morning strikes upon the window bleeding sunlight like there's no tomorrow, like there'll never be the cover of darkness again, demanding a view front to the extreme of the hangover refusing to face the day, the hour, the moment of reckoning for the murdered time lost forever in a blackout more final than oblivion. A cat jumps on the clock crashing it to the floor — a voice whispers from the kitchen . . . "pass the butter please"

Empty Eyes

Those empty eyes setting upon you; they see
nothing of what you are —
A phantom dressed in flesh, you may as well be;
a spiritless entity void of mind and heart, faceless
without shadow to the empty eyes setting upon you
that see nothing of what you are, of all that you are.

World Song

The world is killing, it does not love —
unless Love is blood dripping from
a lion's mouth, or a lamb bleating in
the jaws of a wolf . . .
Fatal is the myth that stretches its lie
to the heart of man, crawling from the
cave of yesterday's dawn still on its belly

Truce

Truce stands dead center in the field
of Commitment awaiting its betrayal.
It will come — it will surely come.
The soldiers of Treachery will see to it.
Truce will not flee from its fate —
it has been through this before.
(Has it ever been through anything else?)

Where Lightning Strikes

Everything sublime, profound, spiritually beautiful and everlasting is born in the silence of solitude.
Thunder claps, lightning strikes, and the heavens pour forth their blessings.

Waiting for the Lightning

just waiting for the lightning . . .

ABOUT THE AUTHOR

Carroll Blair is an award-winning author of more than twenty books. His work has been well endorsed and commendably reviewed, as illustrated by the following commentary from Midwest Review, which proclaimed, "*The poetic expression of Carroll Blair is both unique and compelling. Using word images like the strokes of a painter's brush, Blair creates a resonating recognition that is the mark of a master poet.*"
He is an alumnus of the Boston Conservatory and lives in Massachusetts.

www.ingramcontent.com/pod-product-compliance
Lightning Source LLC
Chambersburg PA
CBHW020010050426
42450CB00005B/406